THE DESIGNER SAYS

Also available in the Words of Wisdom series:
The Architect Says   *The Chef Says*   *The Filmmaker Says*
Laura S. Dushkes   Waxman & Sartwel   Jamie Thompson Stern

The Musician Says   *The Inventor Says*   *The Writer Says*
Benedetta LoBalbo   Kevin Lippert   Kevin Lippert

Published by
Princeton Architectural Press
A McEvoy Group company
202 Warren Street, Hudson, New York 12534
Visit our website at www.papress.com.

Editor: Megan Carey
Designer: Elana Schlenker
Series designer: Paul Wagner

Special thanks to: Nicola Bednarek Brower, Janet Behning, Fannie Bushin, Carina Cha,
Andrea Chlad, Benjamin English, Russell Fernandez, Will Foster, Jan Haux, Diane Levinson,
Jennifer Lippert, Jacob Moore, Katharine Myers, Margaret Rogalski, Dan Simon,
Sara Stemen, Andrew Stepanian, and Joseph Weston of Princeton Architectural Press
—Kevin C. Lippert, publisher

Library of Congress Cataloging-in-Publication Data
Bader, Sara, editor of compilation.
The designer says : quotes, quips, and words of wisdom / compiled and edited
by Sara Bader. — First edition.
159 pages ; 19 cm. — (Words of wisdom)
ISBN 978-1-61689-134-3 (hardcover : alk. paper)
I. Design—Quotations. 2. Designers—Quotations. I. Title.
PN6084.D46B33 2013
745.4—dc23

                                                                    2012043667

the
DESIGNER
says

Quotes, Quips, and Words of Wisdom

compiled and edited by Sara Bader

Princeton Architectural Press, New York

L ong before I worked at Princeton Architectural Press, I collected the books published by this small East Village company. In bookstores, I browsed the shelves, looking for the signature logo on the spine. I'd pull out a PAPress book, and invariably it would be one I wanted to own: a collection of illustrated letters from the Smithsonian's archives or a history of the local architecture and traditions of a small fishing village in Newfoundland. The design of the books themselves reflected the integrity of the content: they were as satisfying to read as to hold. This was a place I wanted to work.

I am now fortunate to be a part of this creative community, editing books on visual culture and design. For more than thirty years, PAPress has published hundreds of titles on design, including monographs of both emerging talent and established practitioners, design briefs, and collections of essays. Our extensive library is just a few feet from my desk. I am surrounded by the words of many of the finest designers—and their words can influence the way we see the world.

Over the last few years, I've become somewhat of a nerdy quote collector. When reading, I no longer flag sentences I want to remember and then promptly return the book to the shelf. I've built a quotation library online at Quotenik.com, so I can share those words with others and easily find them again. I believe that a well-framed thought, read or heard at the right time, can change our perspective, even impact the choices we make. Francis Bacon described quotations as "the edge-tools of speech—which cut and penetrate the knots of business and affairs." James Geary, author of *Geary's Guide to the World's Greatest Aphorists*, compared his collection to a "Swiss army knife for the mind."

The Designer Says, the second volume in this series, follows the structure of the inaugural compilation, *The Architect Says*: one quotation per page, each spread a dialog between two designers. Seymour Chwast avoids the color chartreuse, while Wim Crouwel leans on blue; Sara De Bondt and Carin Goldberg address the necessity of collaboration; and Bruce Mau encourages designers to imitate, but Fabien Baron disagrees ("it's dangerous to get close to someone else's work"). Among other topics, the designers in this compendium reflect on the merits of failure; the role of authenticity; the boundaries (or lack thereof) between work and pleasure; how to successfully staff a studio, collect money from clients, and properly acknowledge mentors; the importance of doing crossword puzzles; and their irrepressible love of typography.

I gathered the quotations from interviews, essays, monographs, and other sources. More than a hundred designers—spanning centuries and continents—express their thoughts here. And yet, by necessity, the compendium is incomplete, a sampling of the extraordinary design talent out there, past and present. (Just paring down Saul Bass's treasury of quotations, for example, presented its own challenge.) It's my hope that this collection will offer inspiration (finding out the moment when a young Milton Glaser knew he wanted to become a graphic designer is a personal favorite), as well as concrete, practical advice—a small but sturdy graphic design "Swiss army knife for the mind."

Sara Bader

I WANT TO MAKE BEAUTIFUL THINGS, EVEN IF NOBODY CARES.

Saul Bass (1920–96)

In hindsight, I think I've always been a designer. I was always inquisitive. Even when I was delivering newspapers I wanted to do it quickly, accurately, and make sure the paper landed on the doorstep in a nice line.

Vince Frost (1964–)

I was thrown out of French class for a day because I was in the back of the room drawing a lowercase *k*. It was then that I knew I should go to art school.

Tobias Frere-Jones (1970–)

At the age of fourteen in Parma, Ohio,
I hadn't the faintest idea of how one would
go about getting type set, and so like
a lot of us, I became very good at tracing.
Then one day my dad happened to visit
a trade show where they were giving away
free samples of a hot new product, dry transfer
lettering. He brought me home a single
sheet of Chartpak 36 pt. Helvetica Medium.
To this day, that typeface at that size
and weight has the same effect on me as
hearing "Maggie May" by Rod Stewart.
It was what I was yearning for: Magical
Instant Real Graphic Design in a Can.

Michael Bierut (1957–)

When I first started studying typography, I have to admit I found it tedious. It wasn't until I managed to relate it to my own perception of the world that it started to fascinate me.

Jonathan Barnbrook (1966-)

TYPOGRAPHERS ARE MASONS OF THE PRINTED WORD.

Alan Fletcher (1931–2006)

Get acquainted with the shapes of the type letters themselves. They are the units out of which the structure is made—unassembled bricks and beams. **Pick good ones and stick to them.**

William Addison Dwiggins (1880-1956)

Letters do love one another. However, due to their anatomical differences, some letters have a hard time achieving intimacy.

Ellen Lupton (1963-)

A good alphabet is like a harmonious group of people in which no one misbehaves.

Jan Tschichold (1902–74)

EVERYTHING HANGS ON SOMETHING ELSE.

Ray Eames (1912–88)

My collages are not jigsaw puzzles,
but organisms that grow until
their weight balances their energy.
What should happen next? Which
way does it seem to turn? **I search for
an internal logic within the work.
That logic may become more complex
or turn in on itself. But it is no
more random than a twisting vine.**

Martin Venezky (1957-)

TAKE THINGS AWAY UNTIL YOU CRY.

Frank Chimero (1984-)

The nature of process, to one degree or another, involves failure. **You have at it. It doesn't work. You keep pushing. It gets better.** But it's not good. It gets worse. You go at it again. Then you desperately stab at it, believing "this isn't going to work." And it does!

Saul Bass (1920–96)

We do a lot of groping here. I don't think there are answers. I think there are thoughts.

Muriel Cooper (1925–94)

I read once about the concepts of the lateral idea and the vertical idea. If you dig a hole and it's in the wrong place, digging it deeper isn't going to help. The lateral idea is when you skip over and **dig someplace else.**

Seymour Chwast (1931-)

IT IS IMPORTANT TO USE YOUR HANDS. THIS IS WHAT DISTINGUISHES YOU FROM A COW OR A COMPUTER OPERATOR.

Paul Rand (1914-96)

Whether instructed to stroke ten thousand cycles or even just a few hundred, the computer never complains.

John Maeda (1966-)

IT'S THE PLEASURE IN SLOWLY CRAFTING TOGETHER SOMETHING WHICH ONLY YOU COULD DO. A WHOLE PLAY WOULD GO BY ON THE RADIO WHILE YOU DID ONE SIDE OF A NEWS-SHEET, BECAUSE OF ALL THE PASTING-UP AND NICKING-OVER OF LINE-ENDINGS. THE SPEED OF IT ON A COMPUTER IS UNAPPEALING.

Richard Hollis (1934–)

The tactile qualities of materials, such as tracing- and colored paper, boards, and overlay film that often were a source of inspiration, are no longer deemed an essential component in developing a design. I first became aware of these changes several years ago, when the art supply store closed my account because I did not purchase enough materials to reach the quarterly minimum charge.

Willi Kunz (1943-)

Make your own tools.

Bruce Mau (1959-)

THE BRAIN IS THE MOST DEMOCRATIC TOOL THAT ALL ARTISTS AND DESIGNERS SHARE.

Daniel Eatock (1975-)

You approach each project searching for a dozen great ideas, not just one or two. After about seven designs, you realize there really are infinite ways to look at a problem. I now completely enjoy the process, though I'm keenly aware that all but one of those dozen great ideas will eventually be killed. It's strangely liberating.

Gail Anderson (1962-)

A graphic designer usually makes hundreds of small drawings and then picks one of them.

Bruno Munari (1907-98)

I HAVE A LOT OF FLAT FILES, BUT I JUST STICK SHIT IN THERE AND NEVER LOOK BACK.

Mike Mills (1966–)

I have a bunch of calendars I used
before I went digital. Every once in a while,
I'll open up one from 1991 and look at
all the names and appointments and things
that, at the time, seemed so important.
Meetings that I was really worried about,
things that I was getting calls four times
a day about, and I wonder, "Where did it
all go? Where are they now?" It's so strange,
everything has disappeared. **The only
thing that stays behind is the work.**

Michael Bierut (1957–)

The ego is not supposed
to be involved in graphic design.
But I find that for myself,
without exception, the more
I deal with the work as something
of my own, as something that is
personal, the more successful
it is as something that's compelling,
interesting, and sustaining.

Marian Bantjes (1963–)

I think my work
has too much character
at times and looks
too much like me.
It's hard for me to
get away from that;
it's hard for me
to remove myself
unless I just did flush
left Helvetica on
a white background
all the time.

James Victore (1962-)

To suggest that the way we use Helvetica is an easy way out typographically is ridiculous. Simply ridiculous. We spend an enormous amount of time spacing, lining, and positioning type. The fact that we use only a small variety of typefaces demands a certain discipline, a skillful precision, a focus on the finer details. **It's certainly not a-different-typeface-for-every-occasion attitude. Now, that would be an easy way out.**

Experimental Jetset:
Marieke Stolk (1967–)
Danny van den Dungen (1971–)
Erwin Brinkers (1973–)

The more uninteresting a letter, the more useful it is to the typographer.

Piet Zwart (1885–1977)

There are ten, maybe fifteen very good typefaces, which I can agree with at least. There are 30,000 on the market, of which 29,990 can be sunk in the Pacific Ocean without causing any cultural damage.

Kurt Weidemann (1922–2011)

One of the things I have observed, looking back historically, is how elegant a seventeenth-century book looks. One of the reasons it looks so elegant is because of the restrictions: **there was only one typeface available**, there weren't that many fonts, and virtually all you could do was play with sizes, italics, and so forth. Automatically it looks elegant by today's standards.

Colin Forbes (1928-)

SOME GET DRUNK FROM A CHEAP BOTTLE OF WINE; SOME GET DRUNK BY STUDYING OLD LETTERFORMS.

Hermann Zapf (1918–)

I have such a love
of typography that
I feel like **it's catnip.**
I have to be careful
that it doesn't seduce
me to the point that
I end up resting on the
beauty of lettering.

Abbott Miller (1963-)

If your words aren't truthful, the finest optically letter-spaced typography won't help.

Edward Tufte (1942–)

I remember reading that
during the Stalin years in
Russia that everything labeled
veal was actually chicken.
I can't imagine what everything
labeled chicken was. We
can accept certain kinds of
misrepresentation, such as
fudging about the amount of
fat in his hamburger, but once
a butcher knowingly sells us
spoiled meat, we go elsewhere.
As a designer, do we have
less responsibility to our public
than a butcher?

Milton Glaser (1929-)

NO ONE LOVES AUTHENTICITY LIKE A GRAPHIC DESIGNER. AND NO ONE IS QUITE AS GOOD AT SIMULATING IT.

Michael Bierut (1957-)

There's a fine line between the slickness that modern eyes and modern technology expect and a **faux distressed look** caused by making things deliberately wobbly.

Matthew Carter (1937-)

The trouble with graphic design today is: **when can you believe it?** It's not the message of the designer anymore. Every applied artist ends up selling his or her soul at some point. I haven't done it, and look at me. People call me one of the most famous designers in the world, and I haven't got any money.

Peter Saville (1955-)

I suspect what I'm really against
is what that term "graphic design"
has come to represent, i.e., synonymous
with business cards, logos, identities,
and advertising, and again, simply put,
those are things I'm just not interested in.
To me that idea of "graphic design"
is as far removed from my interests
as being a milkman or a lawyer. In fact,
I'd rather be a milkman.

Stuart Bailey (1973-)

The words graphic designer, architect, or industrial designer stick in my throat, giving me a sense of limitation, of specialization within the specialty, of a relationship to society and form itself that is unsatisfactory and incomplete. This inadequate set of terms to describe an active life reveals only partially the still undefined nature of the designer.

Alvin Lustig (1915–55)

WHAT I DO IS NOT REALLY
TYPOGRAPHY, WHICH I THINK OF AS
AN ESSENTIALLY MECHANICAL
MEANS OF PUTTING CHARACTERS
DOWN ON A PAGE. IT'S DESIGNING
WITH LETTERS. AARON BURNS CALLED
IT "TYPOGRAPHICS," AND SINCE
YOU'VE GOT TO PUT A NAME ON
THINGS TO MAKE THEM MEMORABLE,
"TYPOGRAPHICS" IS AS GOOD
A NAME FOR WHAT I DO AS ANY.

Herb Lubalin (1918–81)

Respect for the content is an absolute requirement in our business, whether it is about baked beans, or the future of mankind, or what you will.

Ken Garland (1929-)

Stellar examples of graphic design, **design that changed the way we look at the world**, are often found in service of the most mundane content: an ad for ink, cigarettes, sparkplugs, or machinery.

Michael Rock (1959–)

It would seem unlikely that a manufacturer of short-lived paperboard boxes could make the slightest cultural impact upon his time. But the facts show that if **even the humblest product is designed**, manufactured, and distributed with a sense of human values and with a taste for quality, the world will recognize the presence of a creative force.

Herbert Bayer (1900-85)

Among the great and elegant design exceptions is a toy produced this year that has swept the country. What is it? A small bouncing ball—the superball.

Charles Eames (1907–78)

**My work is play.
And I play when I design.**
I even looked it up in
the dictionary, to make
sure that I actually
do that, and the definition
of "play," number one,
was "engaging in a
childlike activity or
endeavor," and number
two was "gambling."
And I realize I do both
when I'm designing.

Paula Scher (1948–)

I'D SOONER DO THE SAME ON MONDAY OR WEDNESDAY AS I DO ON A SATURDAY OR SUNDAY. I DON'T DIVIDE MY LIFE BETWEEN LABOR AND PLEASURE.

Alan Fletcher (1931-2006)

If at all possible, don't be the designer and the one who chases the money. It's very difficult not to get emotional if some bastard isn't paying on time for the beautiful job you have made.

Tony Brook (1962-)

DON'T WORRY ABOUT MONEY, DEAL WITH MONEY.

Mike Monteiro (1967-)

To make a living as a freelance designer—believe me—you have to work hard with your mind and with your hand. For you want to earn at least enough money to dress your beloved wife nicely, to feed your children every day, and to live in a house where the rain does not drop on your drawing pad.

Hermann Zapf (1918-)

I'm not a big spender. **I use every paper twice.** I use these yellow memos: I write them not on one side—two sides— and in different colors, to use them to the utmost.

Irma Boom (1960-)

TO SELL WORK I COULD BE PROUD OF, I'VE HAD TO RANT, RAVE, THREATEN, SHOVE, PUSH, CAJOLE, PERSUADE, WHEEDLE, EXAGGERATE, FLATTER, MANIPULATE, BE OBNOXIOUS, BE LOUD, OCCASIONALLY LIE, AND **ALWAYS SELL,** *PASSIONATELY!*

George Lois (1931–)

My greatest fear is that someone will realize that they shouldn't be paying attention to that woman behind the curtain... that someone will realize that I'm a sham.

Bonnie Siegler (1963-)

There isn't a color I wouldn't use, except chartreuse.

Seymour Chwast (1931-)

IF I DON'T KNOW WHAT TO DO, I USE BLUE.

Wim Crouwel (1928–)

I can say that growing up in the '60s exposed me to how color could be used as a primary design element. Yet surprisingly, I always investigate if the solution could be clearly communicated in black and white.

Jennifer Morla (1955-)

Black letter, black leather, black lingerie, black marks, black tie, the black box, black robes, the black frame that turns white paper into an obituary: **the depth of black takes each situation and makes it more so.**

Lorraine Wild (1953-)

There is no other color
that is better than black.
There are many others
that are appropriate
and happy, but those
colors belong on flowers.

Massimo Vignelli (1931-)

The fact that you can create a third color out of two is something that never ceases to excite me. It's nothing less than a miracle!

Karel Martens (1939-)

I did the bloody thing [I ♥ NY] in 1975, and I thought it would last a couple of months as a promotion and disappear.

Milton Glaser (1929-)

We always take the
long view in designing
a logo so that it is
contemporary enough
to reflect its moment yet
not so trendy as to appear
dated before its time.
As the saying goes,
"Nothing dulls faster
than the cutting edge."

Steff Geissbuhler (1942-)

I was giving a lecture at the **ICA**
and talking about attention-grabbers
and "the trouble with advertising"
and other sorts of things, and I said,
"Some attention-grabbers are
irresistible, like this one, for example,"
and **I** took out a fake pistol and fired it.
It's something I would never do now!
This was back in 1964 or '65,
and I think it was a stupid idea and
I would never do it again.

Ken Garland (1929–)

When Albers gave a lecture, he'd invariably trip over himself as he approached the lectern. He'd also drop his notes. Immediate audience sympathy. I saw him do this at least half a dozen times in nine months. Coincidence?

Alan Fletcher (1931–2006)

I try to staff our studio with people who have curiosity and passion. And you must keep a constant lookout for who you might want to hire next, because often the curiosity of our team leads them on to other things. You can't keep brilliance; you let it shine, and then you have to let it go.

Stephen Doyle (1956–)

EXTOL YOUR MENTORS.... THREE PEOPLE RECOGNIZED MY TALENT AND LED ME TO WHAT I DO TODAY. I SPEAK ABOUT THEM OFTEN IN MY LECTURES, AND IN MY BOOKS.

George Lois (1931-)

Having been working now for over fifty years, I can count the good clients on two or three hands. Why they're good is a magical thing: It has to do with wanting to participate in something they don't really understand. Most people are blind. And to be simultaneously very smart and blind— and to recognize it— takes a rare person.

Ivan Chermayeff (1932-)

If a client comes
to you and says that
they're not really
sure what to do,
that's one of the best
relationships you
can possibly have—
when there's an
acknowledgment
of a goal but the path
to the end product
is unknown, and
they're open to the
collaboration.

Abbott Miller (1963-)

I AM INTERESTED IN IMPERFECTIONS, QUIRKINESS, INSANITY, UNPREDICTABILITY.

Tibor Kalman (1949–99)

Sometimes things are beautiful because they work; and sometimes in trying to make things work, you make something beautiful. Both approaches are interesting, but aesthetics are not our priority. You might say we're interested in the form of side effects.

Dexter Sinister:
David Reinfurt (1971-)
Stuart Bailey (1973-)

If there is something in common about my books, it is the roughness; they are all unrefined. Very often there is something wrong with them.

Irma Boom (1960-)

I LIKE UGLY, RAW WORK.

Barbara deWilde (1962-)

My M.O. became about trying stuff and not worrying about the grid or the structure until I have a feeling for what I'm doing. Then you tidy it up after. If you start off tidy, it's really hard to get messy.

April Greiman (1948-)

Once you've mastered the rules, you can do anything, even abolish them, but without structure it's impossible to get started.

Ed Fella (1938–)

THE PAGE GRID IS THE BASIC SKELETON FROM WHICH YOU HANG EVERYTHING. IT'S EQUIVALENT TO THE SCAFFOLDING, OR THE WALLS AND THE JOISTS OF A BUILDING. A GRID IS CRUCIAL.

Neville Brody (1957–)

The grid system is an aid, not a guarantee.

Josef Müller-Brockmann (1914-96)

We use grids in our work, but we think we use them in a completely different way than, for example, Swiss late-modernist designers, such as Josef Müller-Brockmann. Although we really admire grid-driven work, we wouldn't dare to call ourselves proper gridniks.

Experimental Jetset:
Marieke Stolk (1967-)
Danny van den Dungen (1971-)
Erwin Brinkers (1973-)

I AM A REAL GRIDNIK.

Wim Crouwel (1928–)

I HATE MESSY OFFICES.
I WANT CLEAN TOILETS.
I WON'T HAVE POSTERS ALL
OVER THE PLACE. I WON'T
HAVE CRAPPY NOTICES NEXT
TO THE TOILETS; THAT
ANNOYS ME. WE DON'T PRINT
OUT STUFF IN COMIC SANS,
AND EVEN OUR OFFICE
PEOPLE IN BERLIN KNOW
THAT WHEN THEY PRINT
OUT A NOTICE, THEY MUST
USE OUR STUDIO TYPEFACE.

Erik Spiekermann (1947–)

I love my studio.
It is located above
a Dunkin' Donuts
in an old neglected
four-story building at
14th Street and 6th
Avenue in Manhattan.
It's relatively cheap
by New York standards,
which allows me more
latitude in the work
I'm doing. It's a dump,
but it's my dump.

Paul Sahre (1964-)

OUR STUDIO IS LIKE A DESIGN LABORATORY, AND EVERYONE IS TRYING TO PROVE A THEORY, OR EXERCISE AN EQUATION.

Stephen Doyle (1956–)

MY DREAM IS TO HAVE PEOPLE WORKING ON USELESS PROJECTS. THESE HAVE THE GERM OF NEW CONCEPTS.

Charles Eames (1907-78)

Hire people for what they can teach you, not for what you can teach them.

Rob Giampietro (1978–)

I've had many truly talented designers on my staff because I know I am only as good as the designers I work with, so I see the hiring component as the most important part of my job.

Janet Froelich (1946-)

My first job was as a cleavage retoucher. There was an office meeting about stopping Howard Hughes from showing voluptuous parts of the human body, so I was responsible for taking away the cleavage, not putting it in as they do today.

Ed Benguiat (1927-)

YOU HAVE TO MAKE THE TIME YOU SPEND DOING SOMETHING AS INTERESTING AND AS CONSIDERED AS THE THING ITSELF.

Dexter Sinister:
David Reinfurt (1971-)
Stuart Bailey (1973-)

No one ever built or ruined a career on any piece of work. In the scheme of things, one's failures or successes, for that matter, don't count for a hell of a lot. A sustained body of failures or successes is another matter.

Louis Danziger (1923-)

**When a project fails,
we take as our starting point
the principle that it's
a conversation that didn't
work out the way it should
have, but that doesn't change
anything from the fact
that we made an effort to
serve an idea we believed in.**

Michael Amzalag (1968-)

I'M OFTEN ASKED FOR ADVICE ON HOW TO BECOME A BETTER GRAPHIC DESIGNER, AND THIS IS MY RESPONSE: "TWO THINGS—LEARN HOW TO DO CROSSWORD PUZZLES, AND LEARN HOW TO WRITE."

Chip Kidd (1964–)

READ. TRAVEL. READ. ASK. READ. LEARN. READ. CONNECT. READ.

Erik Spiekermann (1947–)

The good thing about package design is that research is easy—just go into any supermarket or, better yet, any specialty food store. These are my museums.

Louise Fili (1951-)

THROUGH VISITS TO MUSEUMS/SITES/ INSTITUTIONS, READING, RESEARCH, SKETCHING, NOTE TAKING, PHOTO TAKING, AND A GENERAL THREE-WEEK IMMERSION, I FIND MY WAY TO A STORY.

Maira Kalman (1949-)

I write to figure out what I can't make in the studio; I make work in the studio to try to figure out how to engage bigger ideas about design—the ones I can't quite reach in my writing or get to so directly. And when all else fails, I have a painting studio in my basement that is my true sanctuary.

Jessica Helfand (1960-)

Writing is torture for me, but I've forced myself to do it anyway. I felt that it was the best vehicle I had to try to record the experiences I have had as a designer during what I knew were remarkable times. And I knew from my design history research that some of the rarest documents are those of designers speaking in the first person.

Lorraine Wild (1953–)

JUST WHAT IS A BOOK, ANYMORE, ANYWAY?

Craig Mod (1980-)

THE NEW BOOK DEMANDS THE NEW WRITER. INKPOT AND QUILL-PEN ARE DEAD.

El Lissitzky (1890-1941)

I DESIGN LIKE A WRITER AND WRITE LIKE A DESIGNER.

Abbott Miller (1963-)

Designers also trade in storytelling. The elements we must master are not the content narratives but the devices of the telling: typography, line, form, color, contrast, scale, weight, etc. We speak through our assignment, literally between the lines.

Michael Rock (1959–)

Spacing is vital but should be discrete to the point of imperceptibility.

Otl Aicher (1922-91)

Not everyone recognizes
the importance of inner forms,
the shape of the negative
white spaces within the letter.
A perfect letter always
shows beautiful inner spaces.
These must be as uncluttered,
simple, and noble as the
movement and silhouette
of the black shapes.

Jan Tschichold (1902-74)

Letters are peculiar things, and readers can take quite a bit. It is possible to create shapes that are individually unrecognizable as letters but that are readable when put in context.

Erik van Blokland (1967-)

The thing that fascinated
me about Blackletter forms
was the similarity of shapes:
the characters would only differ
very slightly, yet they would
make up all of the meanings,
tones, and variations in language.
It was amazing that out of
this morass of vertical lines,
you could read meaningful text.

Jonathan Barnbrook (1966-)

The twenty-six letters
have been part of our memory
since early childhood.
By themselves, however,
letters lack meaning and are
incapable of transmitting
information. Combined into
a word, a series of letters
can be very powerful, more
precise than a picture.

Willi Kunz (1943-)

I THINK THE REVOLUTION IN TYPOGRAPHY HAS BEEN IN TERMS OF IMAGE. THE PICTURE AND THE WORD HAVE BECOME ONE THING.

Robert Brownjohn (1925–70)

The story of how I decided to become an artist is this: When I was a very little boy, a cousin of mine came to my house with a paper bag. He asked me if I wanted to see a bird. I thought he had a bird in the bag. He stuck his hand in the bag, and I realized that he had drawn a bird on the side of a bag with a pencil. I was astonished! I perceived this as being miraculous. At that moment, I decided that was what I was going to do with my life. **Create miracles.**

Milton Glaser (1929-)

Where I grew up, I always say that the only time I ever heard the word *art* was if you were talking about somebody named Arthur.

Charley Harper (1922–2007)

As far back as I can remember, I loved to make things. I made my own coloring books, I made my own paper dolls, I made dioramas, and I even tried to make my own perfume by crushing rose petals into baby oil....I even handmade an entire magazine when I was twelve with my best friend. Her name was Debbie also, and we named the magazine *Debutante*. We were very proud of it.

Debbie Millman (1961-)

I DON'T KNOW EXACTLY
WHEN MY LOVE FOR CHARTS
BEGAN. I HAVE A CHERISHED
BOOK FROM MY CHILDHOOD
CALLED *COMPARISONS* THAT
HOLDS HUNDREDS OF PAGES OF
CHARTS AND MEASUREMENTS
AND LISTS OF DATA ABOUT
THE FASTEST CARS AND TALLEST
WATERFALLS AND LARGEST
ANIMALS, WHICH DEFINITELY
EXERTED AN INFLUENCE ON ME.

Nicholas Felton (1977-)

IMITATE. DON'T BE SHY ABOUT IT. TRY TO GET AS CLOSE AS YOU CAN. YOU'LL NEVER GET ALL THE WAY, AND THE SEPARATION MIGHT BE TRULY REMARKABLE.

Bruce Mau (1959–)

I don't really look at other people's work.…On the whole I'm influenced by other things— by painters or signs in the street. The way people write "On Sale Now" in shop windows attracts me more than the most serious design. It's not that I don't find anyone good. But I think **it's dangerous to get close to someone else's work and swallow it.**

Fabien Baron (1959-)

I've been described as not having any recognizable style and that's one of the greatest compliments I could hope for. I want each book to have as much of its own individual personality as possible, based on what it is and what it's about.

Chip Kidd (1964-)

I'VE ALWAYS BEEN MORE INTERESTED IN ATTRACTING ATTENTION TO THE PAGE THAN BRINGING ATTENTION TO MYSELF.

Ruth Ansel (1938-)

The "coffee-table" book
is little more than an
extended color-supplement.
Such books—large, thick,
squarish, and trendy,
printed a soupy offset,
plastic-covered, and lavish
with art photography—
such books are a menace
to design students.

Norman Potter (1923–95)

MOST BIG BOOKS ARE CRAP.

Stefan Sagmeister (1962–)

THE PRINTED SURFACE, THE INFINITY OF BOOKS, MUST BE TRANSCENDED. THE ELECTRO-LIBRARY.

El Lissitzky (1890-1941)

The prospect of
change brought about
by the swift flow
of information has
now become so great
that we cannot
find a point to rest—
we're not given a
still picture to
contemplate at leisure.

Quentin Fiore (1920-)

I can concentrate anywhere.
I have a busy open plan studio
with twenty-six people constantly
grabbing me for involvement
in projects, meetings, etc. I have
three small children who wake
up in the middle of the night and
do the same thing.

Vince Frost (1964-)

I think a good place to design is in the cab returning from a meeting. You're infused with the problem, and there's no interference or telephones ringing, and you don't have to talk to the driver. You can just think. It's a very intense fifteen or twenty minutes.

Ivan Chermayeff (1932–)

BY LIVING AND WORKING IN THE
COUNTRY, I FELT I COULD ENJOY A
MORE INTEGRATED LIFE, AND ALTHOUGH
I STILL NEED THE PERIODIC STIMULATION
OF NEW YORK CITY, THE OPPORTUNITY
AND CREATIVE ACTIVITY IN AN AREA OF
BOTH BEAUTY AND TRANQUILITY SEEMED
TO ME TO FAR EXCEED ANYTHING THAT
A STUDIO AND RESIDENCE IN NEW YORK
MIGHT OFFER—THE WAY A MAN LIVES
IS ESSENTIAL TO THE WORK HE PRODUCES.
THE TWO CANNOT BE SEPARATED.

Lester Beall (1903-69)

Our working and home lives are fully integrated. There's no time clock to punch after we climb the two flights of stairs in the morning to the top floor of our house where our offices are. We may be working while the laundry is spinning. Zuzana may be busy with some tricky kerning issues while she has a cake in the oven. The work we create, our photos and ceramics, are all over our house. I often have a basketball game on in the evening while I'm working on my type specimen booklets.

Rudy VanderLans (1955-)

In the right hands, technical constraints turn into celebrations of simplicity, and awkward alphabets are typographic heroes for the day. There is no bad type.

Erik Spiekermann (1947-)
E. M. Ginger (1948-)

I have a fantasy in which I become Type Czar of the World and eradicate all the bad ones.

Seymour Chwast (1931–)

God protect us from the **vagrant** creativity of the typomaniacs.

Kurt Weidemann (1922–2011)

I AM TYPE!

Frederic Goudy (1865–1947)

Every typeface wants to know: "Do I look fat in this paragraph?" It's all a matter of context. A font could look perfectly sleek on screen, yet appear bulky and out of shape in print. Mrs. Eaves has a low waist and a small body.

Ellen Lupton (1963–)

Neither Garamond nor Caslon nor Baskerville ever possessed a bold version before their twentieth-century revival. They were designed and cut in roman and italic only. To use them for modern publicity, in large sizes and set to wide measures, can be brutal. To enlarge Garamond beyond the largest size cast in metal destroys its intimacy.

Emil Ruder (1914-70)

IN ANCIENT TIMES CAPITAL LETTERS (THE ONLY LETTERS IN USE THEN) WERE DRAWN WITH A SLATE PENCIL OR WERE INCISED WITH A CHISEL. THEIR FORM WAS INTIMATELY ASSOCIATED WITH THESE TOOLS.

Herbert Bayer (1900–85)

Handmade engraving
and printing are things of
the past, and while they have
not yet become anachronisms,
their proper place should
be on the dusty shelves of
snobbish collectors.

Alexey Brodovitch (1898–1971)

I often battle with the paper. While I could never work with a crow quill, a Speedball pen or Rapidograph enables me to bear down on the paper.

Seymour Chwast (1931–)

The most beautiful thing is a blank sheet of paper before you put a pencil or pen to it.

Ed Benguiat (1927-)

I don't launch a message
at my viewers but instead
provide an empty vessel.
In turn, I expect them
to deposit something there,
their own messages or images.
This is an important aspect
of communication, accepting
what the other has to say.

Kenya Hara (1958-)

Design is a way of
looking at the world.
You produce an artifact
or create a system
with a set of conditions,
an infrastructure
or an apparatus where
you've done half the
equation and you leave
the rest for whoever
wants to participate.

Lucille Tenazas (1953-)

Designers have always wanted to change the world—it's hardwired in our DNA. Maybe it's time to collectively organize our efforts to really begin to make those contributions. In the meantime, our little enterprise will continue just for the joy of the effort.

William Drenttel (1953-)

MY WORK CONTINUES TO BE CENTERED ON MAKING A PLACE FOR WHO AND WHAT IS LEFT OUT, LISTENING TO THE OTHER PERSON, AND BEING NOT ONLY RECEPTIVE TO CHANGE BUT INITIATING CHANGE.

Sheila Levrant de Bretteville (1940-)

I'm trying to find a way of working which reduces the number of layers of assholes between me and the public.

Tibor Kalman (1949–99)

MOST PEOPLE HAVE SOMETHING POSITIVE TO OFFER, EVEN IF IT IS TOTAL RESISTANCE.

Andrew Blauvelt (1964-)

Having a husband as your client is pretty easy. You never show them what you're doing until late at night. They're exhausted, and they say, "I like it!"

Elaine Lustig Cohen (1927-)

It's a total collaboration…. We do everything together, so we're in a lock-step throughout the process. She's remarkable. **What can I tell you? I love the lady.** I love her for who she is, and I love her for what she does.

Saul Bass (1920-96)

I TRY NOT TO HAVE A STYLE, ALTHOUGH I HAVE ONE! THAT'S WHY COLLABORATION IS IMPORTANT.

Sara De Bondt (1977–)

I thrive on collaboration
and learned early on
as an aspiring painter
in art school that I couldn't
picture myself poor and
alone in a cold garrett
smoking unfiltered Camels.
I need heat, hot water,
nice linens, and the sound
of two hands clapping.

Carin Goldberg (1953-)

Every once in a great while I think I might like to go back to painting.

Janet Froelich (1946–)

I NEVER GAVE UP PAINTING, I JUST CHANGED MY PALETTE.

Ray Eames (1912–88)

I'm fifty-one years
of age now! People still
phone and ask me if
I want to design album
covers. They tell me
I can do whatever I want,
but it's very difficult
for me to explain that
the rack of a record store
is not where I wish to
express myself. Go ask
a twenty-year-old.

Peter Saville (1955–)

YOU CAN'T DO THE SAME THING FOR FIVE YEARS. YOU HAVE TO GET RID OF IT. IT DOESN'T MATTER ANYMORE. JUST LET IT GO, EVEN IF IT'S YOUR SIGNATURE. EVEN IF EVERYBODY EXPECTS YOU TO DO IT. TRY TO FIND ANOTHER WAY TO WALK.

Paula Scher (1948-)

**Little by little, I introduced change
to every aspect of jacket design.
I rejected traditional Pantone colors,
opting to use paint chips from hardware
stores—to the consternation of
my printers. I also cut deals with the
production department, like trading an
extra color for an unusual paper stock.
Book buyers began to take notice.**

Louise Fili (1951-)

Every time I am told that something "must" be done in such and such a way, I eventually find out that the "must" doesn't hold quite the weight it's meant to.

Alvin Lustig (1915–55)

Somehow I am always over my head, or underwater, or inexpert at what I am asked to do. It is thrilling. This is what keeps me coming into the studio every day. You just never know who is going to call and what obstacle they are going to throw in your path.

Stephen Doyle (1956-)

What counts is the present. And that is humbling because no matter how much experience you have, the blank page is still terrifying.... There's fun, anxiety, and concern. But in the end, it's so wonderful when you do make it happen. You live in a sort of threatened state, and then it's delicious when you get out of the danger zone.

Saul Bass (1920-96)

I am already at work on the type of the future.

Lucian Bernhard (1883-1972)

Sincere appreciation to Megan Carey, editor and close friend, for her sharp editorial eye and insight, and for shaping the material every step of the way. I couldn't have asked for a better collaborator. I'm grateful to Elana Schlenker for her excellent design work and always-incisive editorial contributions. Thanks, too, to Paul Wagner and Jan Haux for conceiving the design blueprint for the series and for their collective research advice, and to Janet Behning for her close attention to every detail. To all my colleagues at Princeton Architectural Press, past and present: thanks for the endless inspiration. Special gratitude to publisher Kevin Lippert and editorial director Jennifer Lippert for the opportunity to research this collection and to work on books I love every day.

And to the designers included in this collection: thank you for your words.

Everyone complains that it has all been done before, but we haven't even begun. There's an incredible amount of new tricks up good people's sleeves.

Tibor Kalman (1949–99)